TRAPPED
IN THE
CLOSET

ISBN 979-8-9914777-2-7
Library of Congress Control Number 2025914984

Book Design by NRK Designs

Published by

Cutting Edge Press

TRAPPED
IN THE
CLOSET

IF DIDDY AND R. KELLY BECAME CELLMATES

A Satirical Collection of
Poems
BY RHYME GRIME

Cutting Edge Press

*The book is dedicated
to myself*

Because only Rhyme Grime could rhyme this grime.

Chapter One

JAILHOUSE CONFESSION

Jailhouse Confession

It was a quarter past two when the guards did their rounds
Diddy and R. Kelly in the cell, tryin' not to make a sound
Diddy said, "Bro, I swear, we gon' find a way out"
But the door slammed shut, and the lights went out

Then I looked over, said, "Man, what's that smell?"
He said, "I think that's baby oil—who left it in the cell?"
I started freakin', breathin' heavy, sayin' "This ain't right"
He said, "Calm down, man, we just gotta make it through the night"

But then I heard footsteps, slow and deliberate
He grabbed that baby oil, thinkin' it's gettin' serious
I whispered, "Quick—get in the closet, hide"
Now two grown men in a closet tryin' not to collide

Trapped in the closet, in this jailhouse hell
With a bottle of baby oil and a secret to tell
Can't breathe, can't think, hearts racin' like a train
Two men in the dark, tryin' not to go insane

Sweat drippin' down as the keys start to jingle
He whispered in my ear, "I hear the warden's single..."
I said, "Man, focus—this is no time to flirt"
Then I slipped on the oil and it stained my shirt

The door creaked open, shadows on the floor
I prayed to the Lord they wouldn't look behind the door
He held his breath, I clenched my fist tight
Two convicts in a closet, wonderin' how we got in this plight

Then the light flicked on and the warden called our name
He said, "Y'all boys in there? You oughta be ashamed"
He pulled the door wide, saw the baby oil mess
And he said, "You two explain this—God knows the rest..."

Trapped in the closet, in this jailhouse hell
With a bottle of baby oil and a story to tell
Can't hide, can't run, can't deny what's true
Two men in the dark, got nothin' to lose

So we stepped out slow with our heads hung low
He said, "Lord have mercy, I don't wanna know..."
And as they dragged us out, we tried to save our pride
Two men, one closet, nowhere left to hide.

Chapter Two

JAILHOUSE SCANDAL

Jailhouse Scandal

It was 3 in the mornin', the sirens started to wail
Diddy and R. Kelly locked up in this dirty-ass jail
I said, "Man, why you smilin'? What you got in your hand?"
He said, "A bottle of baby oil—time to execute the plan..."

I said, "What the hell you talkin' 'bout? You losin' your mind?"
He winked, said, "Trust me, bro—tonight, we leavin' it behind."
He twisted off the cap, poured it all on the floor
Slipped on it instantly, hit his head on the door

Now he's laid out cold, baby oil everywhere
I'm standin' in the closet in my underwear
The guard's comin' down, keys janglin' like doom
Two fools in a jail cell, smellin' like a toddler's room

We're trapped in the closet, dark as a tomb
Baby oil glistenin' in this filthy room
Can't scream, can't run, can't cover our tracks
Two men in a nightmare, no turnin' back

The warden peeked in, sayin', "What's all this noise?"
I thought about my mama and my long-lost toys
Diddy woke up moanin', slippin' in the slick
I prayed to the heavens, "Lord, get me outta this quick"

Then the warden stepped closer, pulled out his baton
I knew right then, all our innocence was gone
He said, "Son, explain why you hidin' in there
And why your cellmate's half-naked, baby oil in his hair"

I stuttered and I stammered, tried to make up a lie
But Diddy started singin'—he's a psycho, that guy
He said, "Warden, we was practicin' for a magic escape!"
I just shook my head, knew our fate was shaped

Still trapped in the closet, lost all control
Baby oil drippin' right into my soul
No hope, no chance, no story to sell
Two men in a closet, goin' straight to hell

Then the lights flickered out, and the warden disappeared
I swear to God, man, the whole jailhouse cheered
Diddy started laughin' like the Joker unleashed
I thought, "When I get out, I'm joinin' a priest"

So remember my story, if you ever do time
Don't trust no cellmate with a slick little crime
If you hear that jingle, better say your goodbye
'Cause the closet and the baby oil never lie

Chapter Three

THE BABY OIL INCIDENT (VERSION ONE)

The Baby Oil Incident

It was half past midnight in Cell Block 9
I heard the lock click shut, knew I was outta time
Diddy in the corner with that sinister grin
He said, "Boy, come close—let the madness begin..."

I said, "Man, don't play—what you hidin' behind your back?"
He pulled out baby oil in a greasy old sack
I felt my stomach drop straight through the floor
Two men in a closet—don't know what's in store

The warden's boots echoed down the hall
Baby oil drippin' down the iron wall
Diddy started hummin' like he'd lost his mind
I knew right then, we was runnin' outta time

Trapped in the closet, slippin' in sin
Baby oil glistenin' on my trembling skin
Can't scream, can't breathe, can't even stand
Two fools in the dark with fate in their hands

Then the door swung wide with a blinding glare
The warden stepped in with a thousand-yard stare
He said, "What's this circus I'm lookin' upon?
Two grown men marinated like prawns?"

I tried to explain but my voice gave out
Diddy just giggled, started twistin' about
He poured that oil like a preacher with wine
Said, "Slide with me, brother—leave your old life behind!"

We slipped through the cell in a slick ballet
Like a couple oiled-up seals that lost their way
The guards all screamed, "Contain that mess!"
As we skated down the hall in pure distress

Still trapped in the closet—soaked to the bone
Baby oil nightmares carved in stone
No redemption, no place to hide
Two men on a slipstream ride

Then a rat in a warden's cap appeared in the gloom
He squeaked, "Y'all doomed—this closet's your tomb!"
Diddy yelled, "Follow him—he knows the way!"
I said, "Lord above, get me outta this day!"

We slid through the pipes to a hidden hall
Saw baby oil paintings all over the wall
Portraits of convicts lost to the slick
A whole generation gone too quick

Drip... drip... drip...
It's the sound of regret
A thousand oil bottles
You never forget

Trapped in the closet—forever unclean
Baby oil haunts my every dream
Can't wash it off, can't break the spell
Two men in the closet, descended to hell

And if you're listenin', thinkin' this is a joke...
Don't bring no baby oil...
Behind no cell block cloak...

Chapter Four

THE BABY OIL INCIDENT (VERSION TWO)

The Baby Oil Incident
(Version Two)

It was four in the mornin', the cell smelled like doom
me and Diddy in a closet, in that tiny-ass room
I said, "Diddy, what the hell, how'd we end up in here?"
He said, "Shhh—don't move—if they find us, we're dead,
do you hear?"

Then I slipped on somethin' slick, fell flat on my face
I looked down in the dark—baby oil all over the place
Diddy whispered, "I brought it for... reasons I can't explain..."
I said, "Man, you insane—this is worse than the chain gang!"

The guard dogs barkin', footsteps drawin' near
Closet smellin' like Johnson's, I'm drownin' in fear
The baby oil drippin' from the shelf like tears
Two grown men in a closet, lost all our years

Trapped in the closet, baby oil on the walls
Hearts beatin' fast, hearin' death in the halls
No excuse, no plan, no way to survive
Closet of shame—won't get out alive

Then the warden kicked in the door, eyes wide as hell
Lookin' at the scene like we cast a dark spell
He said, "What the—what is this slippery sight?
Two men oiled up, hidin' out in the night?"

Diddy started singin' like a demon possessed
Said, "Warden, this baby oil—helps relieve the stress!"
I just closed my eyes, waitin' for the end
Covered in oil, betrayed by my cellmate friend

Then the lights flickered red, and the sirens blared
I swear I saw a ghost warden float down the stairs
Diddy poured the last of the oil on the ground
Said, "Slide with me, brother—we'll slip right outta town!"

We slid down the hall like two greased-up fools
Like evil penguins breakin' all the rules
The guards started shootin', we slid through the door
Straight into solitary, forevermore

Trapped in the closet, trapped in our sin
Baby oil-covered from our toes to our chin
No redemption, no grace, no chance to atone
Two men in a closet, now ghosts in the zone

Then the lights cut off, and everything froze
I heard heavy breathin' and a voice that rose
It was the warden, with his ghostly glare
Sayin', "You two slippery bastards—you ain't goin' nowhere…"

Diddy started screamin', tried to slide away
But the floor was so slick, he just spun in place
I crawled to the door, leavin' trails behind
Feelin' like a snail in a cursed oil brine

Then a rat walked by, with a tiny gold crown
He said, "Follow me, fools—if you wanna get outta town"
I said, "Jesus, Mary—what the hell did you bring?
This baby oil got me seein' rodents that sing!"

Still trapped in the closet, can't deny what we've done
Two men and a rat on the slickest prison run
No hope, no logic, no reason or plan
Just baby oil madness in a dark wasteland

The rat led the way through a secret grate
Diddy slid behind me like a greasy fate
We tumbled through tunnels where the dead men moan
Baby oil drip-drip on ancient bones

Finally we emerged in the warden's room
Lit by candles drippin' sulfurous gloom
On his desk lay a book called "The Slippery Path"
Diddy said, "Bro, that's our destiny—do the math"

I cracked it open, pages oozed with oil
I read the curse aloud, started to recoil
It said, "Those who slip shall forever slide
No rest for the wicked—no place to hide..."

Still trapped in the closet—can't get clean
Baby oil nightmares haunt every dream
Two men condemned by a greasy mistake
Now prisoners of slickness, no escape to make

Then the warden's ghost rose up in flame
He said, "Welcome to the legend—you've earned your shame"
He poured more oil as he laughed from the void
Two men in a closet, eternally destroyed

And if you think this is just a tale to amuse...
Remember:
Baby oil...
Don't play with it in county blues...

Chapter Five

THE RAT
BECOMES KING

The Rat Becomes King

It was midnight again when the darkness stirred
I heard tiny footsteps and a whispering word
Me and Diddy thought the nightmare was done
But the rat in the warden's hat had only begun

He scurried on the railing with a crown of bone
His eyes lit up red like a demon enthroned
He squeaked, "All you fools thought you'd break the chain—
But the kingdom of oil still flows through your veins..."

Diddy said, "Oh hell—this ain't real, it can't be..."
But the rat raised his paw and the locks turned free
Hundreds of rodents poured out from the vents
The prison shook as they claimed their vengeance

The Rat becomes King—bow to the throne
A legion of vermin, reclaiming their own
No redemption, no final reprieve
Once you taste the oil, you never leave

He squeaked out commands in a voice so cold
"Bring me the humans who thought they were bold—
You tried to escape, to deny my reign
Now you'll slip forever in an endless chain..."

The rats formed a circle with their tiny claws
Diddy fell to his knees in the oil-slick gauze
I said, "Rat King—please, we paid our due!"
He laughed, "You ain't even halfway through..."

Then the walls started melting into rivers of grease
The rats built a castle in a twisted caprice
They crowned him in shadows, a tyrant so small
But in that baby oil kingdom, he ruled it all

The Rat becomes King—lord of the slick
A rodent messiah with a vengeance so quick
We cried out for mercy that never came
Trapped in the closet of eternal shame

He rose on a throne made of broken cell keys
Said, "All of you mortals, get down on your knees—
In this house of the damned, there's no final song
Just an oily abyss where you all belong..."

So if you ever hear scratching behind your bed...
If you find baby oil where none should be spread...
Remember this tale—how it all went wrong...
And how the Rat became King all along...

Chapter Six

THE OIL RIVER ESCAPE

The Oil River Escape

It was deep in the night when the walls gave way
The Rat King's laughter still haunts me today
Diddy and R. Kelly chained up in a pit of despair
While rivers of baby oil gurgled everywhere

Then the floor cracked open in a boiling stream
A molten flood of slickness straight outta a dream
Diddy whispered, "This is how it ends..."
But I said, "Nah—this is where it begins..."

We broke off the chains with a rusted old hook
Climbed the oiled-up stones while the prison shook
Rats screeched above like a demon choir
We slid to the river—no choice but to dive

Into the Oil River—we leapt through the flames
Two desperate men with no more names
No law, no warden, no kingdom to claim
Just an endless current of slippery shame

The current pulled us under to a cavernous hole
We passed skeletons of inmates swallowed whole
Diddy cried out, "God, this river's alive!"
I just prayed to the darkness that we'd survive

We surfaced again in a swirling abyss
Rats on rafts with torches hissed
The Rat King pointed with a claw of bone
Said, "Run all you want—you still ain't goin' home!"

Then a wave crashed over, black and deep
I thought of my mama, I started to weep
But Diddy reached out, grabbed hold of my arm
Said, "Brother, we gotta ride this oily storm..."

On the Oil River—no turning back
Two broken souls in a pitch-dark track
No redemption, no pardon, no sweet goodbye
Just a flood of regret in a dead man's tide

We drifted for miles under torch-lit vaults
Past the Rat King's statues and ancient faults
At last, daylight cracked through a sewer grate
One final chance to escape our fate

So we crawled from that river, barely alive...
Covered in oil...
But somehow...
Still free...

But every night, I still hear it flow...
The river beneath the prison...
Calling me home...

Chapter Seven

THE SLIPPERY REDEMPTION

The Slippery Redemption

It was dawn in the dungeon when my eyes cracked open
Baby oil everywhere—like a curse unbroken
Diddy lay snorin' in a puddle of shame
While that rat in the warden's hat whispered my name

He said, "Boy, you been slippin' way too long
But there's a way to atone, to right what's wrong
Beyond the north tunnel lies a cleansing flame
If you can reach it alive, you'll be free of this game"

I crawled to my feet, leavin' greasy tracks
Haunted by the screams from the oil-slick past
Diddy awoke, said, "Redemption? You sure?"
I said, "Bro, anything's better than this oily manure"

This is the Slippery Redemption—our final chance
To wash off the sins of that freak off dance
No more glidin', no more shameful slide
Just a flicker of hope we might survive

We crept through the corridor, the lights burnin' red
I heard the warden's voice echo in my head:
"Once you slip in the oil, you can never get clean
Your soul stays greasy in ways unseen…"

But I kept movin' forward through the grime and tears
Past the shadows of the inmates swallowed by fear
I saw the flame flicker in the warden's vault
I thought, "Lord, forgive me—this ain't all my fault…"

Then Diddy fell down with a desperate cry
Oil in his eyes, sayin', "Leave me to die!"
But I reached for his hand, pulled him through the fire
and the flames burned clean all our dark desires

This is the Slippery Redemption—baptized in flame
Burned off the oil and erased the shame
Two men reborn from a haunted night
Crawlin' out the closet into morning light

We emerged from the dungeon with the dawn on our skin
No more baby oil—no more original sin
The guards just stared as we staggered past
Two men free at last from the slippery past.

So if you ever find yourself lost in the slick...
Remember:
Redemption waits...
But you gotta crawl through the fire to get it...

Chapter Eight

THE FINAL SLIP

The Final Slip

It was dawn on the outskirts, freedom in sight
Diddy and R. Kelly limped forward, caked in the night
Thought we'd left the oil behind in the past
But that slick little river was never outclassed

I heard a whisper float up from the drain
a voice like a curse etched into my brain
"You can't run," it hissed, "You can't repent—
Once you slip in the oil, your soul's for rent..."

Diddy turned 'round, eyes hollow and black
Said, "I feel it pullin' me back..."
I grabbed his hand, but he slipped away
Into a puddle that swallowed the day

This is the Final Slip—no more reprieve
The oil claims all who ever believe
No salvation, no last appeal
Just the endless slide—cold and real

The Rat King emerged in a plume of smoke
With a crown on his head and a voice that broke
"Your story's over, your legend done—
This oil-soaked saga is second to none…"

I tried to crawl, but the ground gave way
Like a trapdoor to hell on judgment day
Diddy was gone, just ripples remain
The Final Slip etched in my veins

I sank in the darkness, no breath to draw
Past the bones and chains and broken law
The river took me with a gentle sigh
And I knew in that moment, I'd never die

In the Final Slip—where all things end
Where the oil and shadows twist and blend
No escape, no dawn, no cleansing flame
Just the river that whispers my name

Some nights in the world above, you might hear
A sloshing sound creeping near your ear
And if you see baby oil on your floor
Lock up tight—don't open your door

Because the Final Slip waits for everyone...
And when it comes...
It's already too late...

Slip...

Slip...

Slip...

Chapter Nine

THE SLIPPERY RESURRECTION

The Slippery Resurrection

I don't know how long I sank in that well
Time didn't matter in that oil-borne hell
but one day I opened my crusted eyes
and saw a flame in the darkness rise

It was Diddy, burning with ghostly light
His silhouette gleaming in the endless night
He cried, "I won't leave you here to drown—
this is our time to turn it around!"

He reached in the pit with a phantom hand
pulled me up from that cursed land
and as I surfaced from the oily tomb
I saw the walls crack across the room

The Slippery Resurrection—against all odds
Two men reborn by the grace of gods
No Rat King decree could hold us down
We rose from the river, unbowed, unbound

The Tribunal screamed as the floor gave way
The oil turned to vapor at the break of day
I felt the chains fall off my chest
Knew at last we'd been cleansed, been blessed

But the Rat King's laughter echoed on...
And I knew the battle wasn't won...

Chapter Ten

THE
RAT KING'S FALL

The Rat King's Fall

We burst through the vault to the warden's keep
Where the Rat King ruled from a throne so steep
He screeched, "You dare defy my reign?
I'll drown you again in the oily bane!"

Diddy picked up a torch of blue flame
Said, "It's over, rodent—remember my name!"
He hurled the fire to the throne of bone
The Rat King shrieked in a deafening tone

Flames danced on the walls of grease
At last, the reign of oil would cease
the rats all scattered to the dark beyond
And the Rat King's power was finally gone

This was the Rat King's Fall—ashes to dust
His kingdom of slime broken and crushed
Two men emerged in the newborn dawn
While the last of the oil burned and was gone

The prison walls crumbled under morning light
the corridors cleansed by fire bright
Diddy fell to his knees in the soot and flame
Said, "Brother, nothing will be the same…"

And I knew he was right…
We had slipped…
But we had survived…

Chapter Eleven

THE
LAST DROP

The Last Drop

Years have passed since that cursed night
since we crawled from the dark into honest light
but every now and then, when I close my eyes
I still hear the river's oily cries

And sometimes...
When the moon is high...
I see a tiny crown in the corner of my room...

Slip...

Slip...

Slip...

And the last drop falls...

Prequel Chapter One

THE BIRTH
OF THE RAT KING

The Birth of the Rat King

Long before I ever knew that cell
before the oil and the closet from hell
There was a shadow under Cell Block Three
Where a rat was born to a twisted decree

They said he was cursed by the warden's wife
Born in the walls to a secret life
Fed on scraps and the warden's sin
until he rose with a crown within

He learned to whisper in the prisoners' ears
To feed their hunger, to stoke their fears
And every time a convict cried
He grew stronger in the dark inside

This is the Birth of the Rat King—born to rule
the patron saint of the oil and the fool
in the prison's veins he learned to creep
until every man bowed low and weeped

He found the storeroom where the baby oil lay
A thousand barrels hidden away
He bathed in the slick for seven nights
Emerging crowned in endless blight

And so the Rat King claimed the dark...
Long before the first man slipped...

Prequel Chapter Two

THE FIRST SLIP

The First Slip

Before my time, before my crime
Another poor fool crossed that line
A funny man named Bill with trembling hands
Who heard the Rat King's oily demands

They said Bill tried to break his chains
By smuggling oil through the warden's drains
But the Rat King caught him in the act
Dragged him down with a smile so cracked

Bill cried, "Lord, don't let me drown!"
But the oil rose up, pulled him down
and when the guards came in at dawn
all that was left was a whisper... gone

This was the First Slip—where the legend grew
The oil claimed the wicked, claimed the true
No trial, no tomb, no final word
Just the Rat King's laugh that no one heard

From that night on, the prison knew
If you smelled baby oil, your days were through
Some say Bill's still in the walls
Waiting to slip you when darkness falls

So don't forget the name of the first who fell...
The oil remembers every tale...

Prequel Chapter Three

THE
HIDDEN RIVER

The Hidden River

Long before Diddy and me were born
The prison was built on a swamp forlorn
The warden's men dug too deep
Found a river of oil that never sleeps

They sealed it up behind iron doors
Wrote its secret in hidden laws
But the Rat King knew where it wound
And spread its curse through the underground

He whispered to the pipes at night
He fed the river with all his might
And when the first storm broke the seal
The oil came pouring—hungry and real

This is the Hidden River—old and cursed
Older than the warden's thirst
Black as sorrow, thick as lies
Where the oil lives and never dies

So when you hear the gurgle low
And feel the floorboards start to go
Remember this river under your feet
It's always waiting for more to eat

Long before our story began...
The river was there...
And the Rat King was watching...

Prequel Chapter Four

THE
WARDEN'S PACT

The Warden's Pact

Back when the prison was first laid in stone
The warden walked these halls alone
He found the river black as night
And struck a deal in the candlelight

He said, "I'll feed you souls and sin
If you grant me power no man can win"
The river whispered back through the iron grate
"Bring me the damned, and seal their fate…"

From that hour, the prison grew
Walls of iron, shadows too
The warden's eyes turned cold as ash
And every convict paid in cash

This was the Warden's Pact—sealed in dread
A river of oil for the lives he bled
No mercy, no pardon, no way to break
The promise made for power's sake

He kept the secret locked away
Buried under brick and clay
But every night he'd feel it rise
The river hungry behind his eyes

And that's how the curse began...
A pact no warden could outrun...

Prequel Chapter Five

THE
OIL BAPTISM

The Oil Baptism

Years later in a hidden hall
The Rat King waited for the final call
A hundred rats in a circle tight
Chanting hymns in the dead of night

They crowned him with a filth-stained wreath
Dipped his body underneath
Into the vat of oil below
Where no sane creature dares to go

He sank in darkness, did not drown
Rose up wearing an oiled crown
Eyes aflame with a hunger wild
No longer rat—no longer child

This was the Oil Baptism—black rebirth
The moment he claimed this prison's worth
Not just vermin, not just beast
But a monarch of the oily feast

When he emerged on the prison floor
The guards all fled and locked the door
But they say no lock can bar his reign
Once the baptism sears your brain

And in that sacred rite...
He became the oil's first and only king...

Prequel Chapter Six

THE
FIRST TRIBUNAL

The First Tribunal

The warden thought he ruled alone
Till the Rat King claimed his throne
He called a meeting in the crypt below
Where no living man should ever go

A tribunal of rats in tattered gowns
Judges of oil, wielders of crowns
They read the charges on a human skull
And the warden felt his courage dull

"You promised souls," the Rat King hissed
"But you hoard the oil for your own bliss
The pact demands a price unpaid—
Tonight, your debt will be repaid..."

This was the First Tribunal—verdict of night
No jury of men, no hope in sight
A sentence passed without a plea
The warden sank beneath the oily sea

When dawn came cold, the guards awoke
To find the throne and warden broke
And from that hour, every man inside
Feared the oil and the Rat King's pride

And that's the secret no guard will tell...
How the Tribunal rose from hell...

Final Epilogue

THE LAST TESTAMENT
OF THE OIL

The Last Testament of the Oil

I sit here in this empty cell
Older now, with tales to tell
My hands still slick, my soul still scarred
By everything I ran from, a haunting affair

I've seen the river no man survives
The Rat King's court, the haunted cries
I've felt the oil rise up my throat
Heard the tribunal's final vote

They say the prison fell one night
The walls gave way to endless blight
A flood of oil that drowned the halls
Turned iron and stone to shadows and calls

This is the Last Testament—the end of the tale
The kingdom of grease where the damned set sail
No warden remains, no Rat King's crown
Just the river of blackness dragging us down

Diddy is gone, but I still dream
Of that slippery hell and its silent screams
Sometimes I wake to a phantom drip
And feel the urge to let myself slip

But I crawl to the mirror and face the past
The cursed river, the pact cast
The Rat King's eyes behind my own
The oil's dark whisper in my bones

This is the Last Testament—my final breath
A confession etched in oily death
If you find this tale, burn the page
Don't let the river out of its cage

Because somewhere...
Beneath your feet...
It still waits...

Slip...

Slip...

Slip...

And that...
Is the end...

Rhyme Grime—
Grime spits bars from the basement of the bizarre.
A lyrical outlaw with a taste for satire and grime.
He crafts stories that blur the line between surreal
horror and lyrical comedy.
Where rhythm meets grime...It's Grime time.